JOY GETS THE LAST WORD

FOLLOWING GOD'S PLAN FOR YOUR LIFE AFTER DIVORCE

CAROL SCHREIBER

WESTBOW
PRESS®
A DIVISION OF THOMAS NELSON
& ZONDERVAN

WestBow Press books may be ordered through booksellers or by contacting:

WestBow Press
A Division of Thomas Nelson & Zondervan
1663 Liberty Drive
Bloomington, IN 47403
www.westbowpress.com
844-714-3454

All Scripture quotations are taken from the King James Version.

ISBN: 978-1-6642-6444-1 (sc)
ISBN: 978-1-6642-6445-8 (hc)
ISBN: 978-1-6642-6443-4 (e)

Library of Congress Control Number: 2022907760

Print information available on the last page.

WestBow Press rev. date: 05/16/2022

CONTENTS

PREFACE

Have you ever had a "cry-out-to-Jesus" moment?

I'm not talking about while driving in your car, someone cuts you off, and you yell out, "Lord, help them to be better drivers!"

The "cry-out-to-Jesus" moment that I'm talking about is a guttural, heart-wrenching, life-changing call to our Savior, whether it be for healing, or decision-making, or something else. In that moment, we know we need Christ, and we call out to Him for help. Flat on our faces, prostrate, hearts screaming out, "I need you, Lord!"

I had that moment days after my divorce was final.

I remember vividly standing on the steps of my beach house. It was nighttime, I was emotional, and I needed our Lord.

The prayer that I prayed that night changed my life. It opened many doors. I'll share the prayer with you shortly. But right now, just know this:

- Our God is bigger than our problems.
- When we pray, we tend to want safety. But God wants excellence.
- Don't limit God when you pray. He is a big God!

God doesn't want your life to just be enough. He wants it to be more than enough. He wants you to have the abundant life (John 10:10). God will show up in your life to teach you that He is more than enough.

I hope this book allows you to find true joy after divorce. I certainly don't think I'm an expert on life after divorce, but I do know that God gave me belly-laughing, life-transforming, serving-Him joy after my divorce. And I can't wait to share with you how He did it!

> I lift my eyes up to the hills. From where does my help come? My help comes from the Lord, who made heaven and earth. (Psalm 121:1–2)

JOY IN DIVORCE

IS "JOY IN Divorce" an oxymoron? It doesn't have to be.

I decided to write this book because I couldn't find any helpful Christian books on life after divorce when I needed one. Most of the books I found at the bookstore were about how to get a man, where to find a man, and how to dress to find a man. None of that interested me. That wasn't my priority. I wanted to move ahead in my new, single life with God at the steering wheel. That was my goal. I sought it, found it, and lived it. My new life's goal was a God-pleasing life postdivorce.

Many people after their divorces don't know what their purpose is. They're drifting and searching, but don't even know what they're searching for. God has a plan and a purpose for our lives. When we are in the center of His will, He will help us be the people He wants us to be. Rest your soul in Him, and you will find your peace and purpose.

I certainly don't want to come across as an advocate for divorce. In fact, let me start off by saying God doesn't want divorce. It's not in His plan for our lives. He is the Author of our life, and He's not writing that chapter.

Divorce separates what God has joined, and He hates that (Matthew 19:6). We should never want to divide what God has unified, especially when it comes to the institution of marriage. Marriage is the one earthly relationship in which God declares the two are now one in His sight (Ephesians 5:31). It is so important to Him that He considers it adultery for a spouse to divorce without biblical grounds and move on to another person.

I believe that deeply, and for years in my troubled marriage, I went through counseling with my spouse, trying to make it work. I didn't want to let God, or my children, down, and I sure didn't want Satan to win. I wanted to live biblically. And most importantly, when I go to Heaven and stand face to face with Christ, I want to be sure that I attempted everything to make my marriage last and tried earnestly to uphold my vows.

But after many attempts at counseling with our pastor, numerous therapists, and non-stop praying to our Father for help and intervention, it was obvious that our marriage wasn't going to work.

As soon as I filed for divorce, the Holy Spirit filled me with complete peace. For me, this was affirmation that I had made the right decision for my children and me. After years of hurt and pain in our house, it was a wonderful feeling to be filled with peace! I looked towards our future with excitement and confidence by putting that future in the Lord's hands.

Biblical Self-Talk

During the months leading up to my divorce being final, I began biblical self-talk. I guess you could say I started talking to myself. It was my coping skill. Let me be clear: I am not talking about motivational talks to myself inspired by New Age gurus. I didn't look at myself in the mirror and say to my reflection, "You are amazing!" I am talking about scriptural self-talk used to glorify God and for the spiritual health of my soul.

Actually there are examples of self-talk all through the Bible. If you look closely, many of the writers of inspired Scripture pen words to themselves.

- In Psalms 42–43, David talks to himself three times with the same basic words. These words were likely written when he was in exile after being banished by the betrayal of his son, Absalom. He is far from home and close to despair. He says to himself, "Why are you cast down, O my soul? And why are you disquieted within me? Hope in God; for I shall yet praise Him, The help of my countenance and my God" (Psalm 42:5, 11; 43:5). David asks himself the reason for his discouragement and the trouble he feels within his soul. He tells himself to put his hope in God so his soul will give praise to God because He can always be counted on to help. David encourages his own heart. He's having a heart-to-heart talk with himself.
- Jeremiah speaks to himself about his sorrow over God's judgement of Judah. He writes, "O my soul, my soul! I am pained in my very heart! My heart makes a noise in me; I cannot hold my peace, because you have heard, O my soul, the sound of the trumpet, the alarm of war" (Jeremiah 4:19). This is part of Jeremiah's way of sorting through the deep emotions of sorrow over a very tragic situation. Yet, through it all, Jeremiah turns to the Lord for comfort in his deep affliction.
- Deborah in Judges 5:21 says to herself, "Oh my soul, march on in strength."

These are great examples of self-talk from the Bible.
For me, self-talk helps in three ways.

1. It helps me evaluate a situation and tweak my mindset.
2. It helps me focus on God and not my condition.
3. It helps me maintain an attitude of thankfulness while putting all my confidence in God.[1]

Here is a real example of how I self-talk

My mind is reeling. Finances are tough this month. I have four children to feed, extra school expenses, and Christmas is coming up. I noticed my car was making a noise *and* there is a drip under my sink.

Using biblical self-talk:

1. I quote to myself a verse that really speaks to me at the time, such as Proverbs 3:5–6: "Trust in the Lord with all thine heart; and lean not unto thine own understanding, in all thy ways acknowledge him, and he shall direct thy paths." I repeat this verse over and over until my mind stops reeling.
2. I assess the situation and realize things *could be worse.* At least I *have* a car (that is making a noise) and a house (that has a drip under the sink).
3. I break down the verse phrase by phrase, like this.
   a. —"Trust in the Lord with all thine heart..." Am I completely and wholly relying upon God? Do I appreciate His goodness and wisdom? Do I accept His promise for direction and help in all areas of my life?
   b. "Lean not to thine own understanding..." Don't think for a second my carnal mind can figure this out on its own.
   c. "In all thy ways acknowledge him..." In everything, know His ways.
   d. "And he shall direct thy paths." God's way is safe and good and will bring me a happy ending.

The more I self-talked, the better I got at it. In time, it became second nature to me, like breathing. Instead of going into panic mode when a situation arose that I wasn't expecting, my mind reacted biblically and I was able to self-soothe my anxieties and fears.

Keep Your Eyes on Jesus

Always, but especially after a divorce, we need to be staring at Jesus. Unblinkingly. Non-stop. When my youngest son, Grant, was a baby, he only wanted me or his dad to hold him. We were his everything. He would cry and cling to us if anyone else tried to hold him. He only felt confident around us. That's how God wants us to be. Clinging to Him. Only confident with Him. He is our whole world. He is our everything. We rely on Him for everything. And in a moving, fluctuating, frenzied world, He is what we know. We can be confident in Him. He alone is what we can depend on.

I always think of Mary at Jesus's feet. I love what Jesus says to Martha when she complains that her sister isn't helping: "'But one thing is needful: and Mary hath chosen that good part, which shall not be taken away from her'" (Luke 10:42). Be the person who refuses to move from Jesus's feet, even when everyone is shouting at you to get things done that the world says are important. By doing so, we will bring God glory by bringing attention to Him.

Many things in this book are the opposite of what the world will tell you. The world will say, "You deserve happiness. It's time for you to put yourself first. Do what *you* want to do. Enjoy yourself. Listen to your heart. Be in control. Be independent. Be footloose and fancy-free. Don't settle for anything less than your dreams."

It can be easy to slip into that mindset when we are bombarded by television, magazines, and the internet all giving us that message. Our culture doesn't want us to follow Jesus. But do not stray from Biblical truth. We are to be dependent on Christ. *He alone is our example.*

> See to it that no one takes you captive by philosophy and empty deceit, according to human tradition, according to the elemental spirits of the world, and not according to Christ. (Colossians 2:8)

Going through a divorce is not easy. It can be a long, tough road. But friend, please listen when I say this. Never stop seeking God through this time. Remember that He is *for* you, not *against* you (Romans 8:31). He will work all things together for good for those who love Him (Romans 8:28). God will redeem every hurt you have experienced.

Many of you may not understand your singleness. You didn't want it or have any control over it. But someday, we will have to give an account to Jesus as to how we used it. Spend your period of singleness as a gift to God. He will be glorified, and any hurt you may have will be transformed to a great thing.

Proverbs 1:33 promises us, "But whoever listens to me will dwell safely, and will be secure, without fear of evil." The key phrase here is *listen to me.* God will lead, and you will follow.

Just as He resurrected his son from the grave, He can resurrect your life from the death of divorce. God has a plan, a future, and a timetable for your life. It will all become apparent in His perfect timing. You simply have to learn how to be patient during these waiting phases.

I have seen God come through time and time again for me without fail. He will do the same for you. You will have a great, abundant life because of Him.

Walking with the Lord gives you pure *joy*!

2

JOY IN PRAYER

The Prayer of All Prayers

REMEMBER IN THE beginning I told you about my "cry-out-to-Jesus" moment? During that moment, I said a prayer that changed my life and doors flew open because of that prayer. Here's what happened.

One night about a week after my divorce was final, I put my kids to bed after hearing their prayers. I cleaned up the kitchen and then went outside to sit on my steps. If I listened closely, I could hear the waves from the Gulf of Mexico half a block away. Summer was here, the kids were out of school, and the long, lazy days were starting. I looked up at the clear, night sky and marveled at the stars. Did you know there are more stars than grains of sand? There are ten times more stars in the night sky than grains of sand in the world's deserts and beaches. Isn't that amazing? Just that day I had gone to the beach with my kids and built a sand castle. I ran my hands through the sand—thousands of grains just in my hand. Supposedly there are two million grains of sand in one cup. That by itself is astonishing. But here's something even more astonishing: *there are even more stars than grains of sand.* When we look up at the night sky, we're only seeing a sliver of them. And guess what?

> He counts the number of the stars;
> He calls them all by name. (Psalm 147:4)

God knows the exact number of stars *and* He calls them all by name. If that doesn't make you marvel at His greatness, I don't know what will.

He created all the stars and placed them exactly where He wanted them. And He knows each of their names. *Wow!*

As I sat on those steps overcome with these thoughts, the Holy Spirit filled me with His overwhelming presence. I was overcome with love for my great God. Any fears I had of being an unemployed, single mom vanished. I thought to myself, *My God is so big! If He knows the stars that well, He knows me even better than that. He's told me He cares about me even more than the birds.* Matthew 6:26–33 is so beautiful and such a comfort.

> "Look at the birds of the air, for they neither sow nor reap nor gather into barns; yet your heavenly Father feeds them. Are you not of more value than they? Which of you by worrying can add one ₁ cubit to his stature? So why do you worry about clothing? Consider the lilies of the field, how they grow: they neither toil nor spin; and yet I say to you that even Solomon in all his glory was not arrayed like one of these. Now if God so clothes the grass of the field, which today is, and tomorrow is thrown into the oven, will He not much more clothe you, O you of little faith?

Therefore do not worry, saying, 'What shall we eat?' or 'What shall we drink?' or 'What shall we wear?' For after all these things the Gentiles seek. For your heavenly Father knows that you need all these things. But seek first the kingdom of God and His righteousness, and all these things shall be added to you."

Right then on that step, I decided the rest of my life was going to be devoted to serving the Lord. Every breath and step was for Him, and Him alone. I didn't know *how* I would do it, or *where* I would do it, or *what* I was going to do, but He did. With every fiber of my being, believing every single word in my heart, I prayed,

> Dear Lord,
> From this day forward,
> I dedicate my life to serving You.
> My life is *Yours*,
> do with it as You will.
> Amen

I didn't restrict God by asking Him to get me a job at XYZ Company. I didn't restrict God by asking Him to put a man in my life. My Creator knows what is best for me. He loves me. Without any hesitation, I just turned myself over to Him. Here you go, Lord. Have my life.

I prayed that prayer with all my heart and with all my might. I wasn't just going through the motions. That's what the Bible tells us. If we are going to sing, let's sing with all our heart; if we are going to study, let's study with all our heart; and if we're going to pray, let's pray with all our heart (Ecclesiastes 9:10).

Now that God was in complete and total control of my life, it took the burden off me. It was now His job to take care of me in every detail. There is no area in my life that He is not willing to help me out with. The Holy Spirit is called "the Helper" in the Bible. It is now His job to help you in every single area of your life where you will need His help.

Because I believe God is sovereign and has my best intentions at heart, I was willing to entrust the nuts and bolts of my daily life into His hands.

Saying a prayer like that, and believing it with all your heart, be ready to have your life turned upside down. We tend to want safety in our life, but God wants excellence. Experiences I never would have sought were about to be offered to me, because God was running the show, and it was amazing. I was ready to conform completely to whatever God's plan was for me. I wanted to live out John 4:34: "My food is to do the will of Him who sent me, and to finish His work."

After praying that prayer, doors started flying open. And I knew every door was opened by *Him*. That prayer was like Miracle Grow on my life. Life after divorce wasn't scary. It took on purpose, meaning, and excitement because I was walking hand in hand with God.

You are the Potter, Lord. I am the clay.

> "But that the world may know that I love the Father, and as the Father gave me commandment, so I do. Arise, let us go from here." (John 14:31)

Prayer Life

So let me ask you this: how is your prayer life? Do you talk frequently throughout the day with our Father? Good relationships thrive on good communication, just like a close relationship with God grows by our prayers.

I am a preschool teacher at a Christian school. I have a class full of three and four year-olds. Adorable, right? I teach them many things and one of them is how to pray. You can tell many of them pray at home with their parents. They ramble on and on—it's so cute. And then there are some who have never prayed before. They freeze when I ask them to pray. So then I rephrase it with, "What do you want to tell God today?" And they stop and think, *What do I want to tell Him?* I've heard all kinds of prayers from my students through the years.

"Dear God...

"Please help my little brother to stop biting me."

"Can you please give me a monster truck for my birthday?"

"Can you fix my TV so I can watch *Frozen* again?"

"Please help my mommy and daddy to talk nicely to each other."

Whatever they pray for, I tell them that praying to God is just *talking* to Him. Whatever is on your heart today, tell God about it.

We can learn how to pray from the best of the best. Jesus was a great example on how to pray. We're not talking about a new believer in Christ here, but Jesus Christ, the Holy One Himself.

1. Jesus made a time and place for prayer.

   Luke 5:16: "So He Himself often withdrew into the wilderness and prayed."

   Matthew 6:6: "But you, when you pray, go into your room, and when you have shut your door, pray to your

Father who is in the secret place; and your Father who sees in secret will reward you openly."

Mark 1:35: "Now in the morning, having risen a long while before daylight, He went out and departed to a solitary place; and there He prayed."

Mark 6:46: "And when He had sent them away, He departed to the mountain to pray."

2. Jesus showed that prayer is necessary. Even when He had the weight of the world upon Him, He stopped and prayed in the Garden of Gethsemane.

Matthew 26:39: "And he went a little further, and fell on his face, and prayed, saying, O my Father, if it be possible, let this cup pass from me: nevertheless not as I will, but as thou wilt."

3. Jesus wants us to pray in all situations, especially when we're tired.

Mark 14:37–38: "And he cometh, and findeth them sleeping, and saith unto Peter, 'Simon, sleepest thou? couldest not thou watch one hour? Watch ye and pray, lest ye enter into temptation. The spirit truly is ready, but the flesh is weak.'"[2]

I'm a morning person. I can conquer the world at 6 am, but leave me alone at 9 pm. I'm usually in bed reading by that time. So mornings have always been my favorite time to spend with the Lord. All I need is my coffee, my Bible, and Jesus to start my day. Prayer calms my soul, draws me closer to the Lord, and keeps me steadfast.

My prayer time has been something I have had to cultivate. When I was younger, I often felt too busy to pray. After all, I had to sleep, work, and take care of my children. If I had any time *left over,* I would give *that* to the Lord. But then I realized I had it all backwards. Without a doubt, I need prayer surely as much as I need food and sleep. After dedicating my life to God and completely relying on Him, I wanted to demonstrate that reliance by harvesting my prayer life.

Now I savor my prayer time with God. It's not hard for me to get out of bed in the morning when I know I'm going to meet my Savior in prayer. Scripture does not command us to pray in solitude, but for me I crave it. It has been a growing process, but I love to be unplugged from the world when it's my Jesus time.

Ruth Bell Graham wrote in her book *Legacy of a Pack Rat,* "We cannot pray and remain the same. We cannot pray and have our homes remain the same. We cannot pray and have the world about us remain the same. God has decreed to act in response to prayer. 'Ask,' He commands us. And Satan trembles for fear we will."[3]

We should pray with a purpose. What needs to be done? When I sit down in the morning, ready to talk to our Father, I often use the tried and true acronym ACTS.

- **Adoration:** Pray to adore the Father by giving Him praise and honor over everything.
- **Confession:** Pray for forgiveness of any sin in your life.
- **Thanksgiving:** Verbalize what you're grateful for in your life for thanksgiving is a mark of a true believer.
- **Supplication:** Pray for the needs of yourself and others.

For me, this works to remember the key elements when I'm praying. But really there is no guideline. Just talk to God. Come before His throne in awe and reverence.

Another reason I love to pray is because God loves to hear our prayers. Isn't that amazing? The Creator of the Universe loves to hear from *us*. He says it is like incense to Him.

> And when he had taken the book, the four beasts and four and twenty elders fell down before the Lamb, having every one of them harps, and golden vials full of odours, which are the prayers of saints. (Revelation 5:8)

> And another angel came and stood at the altar, having a golden censer; and there was given unto him much incense, that he should offer it with the prayers of all saints upon the golden altar which was before the throne. And the smoke of the incense, which came with the prayers of the saints, ascended up before God out of the angel's hand. (Revelation 8:3–4)

Isn't it a beautiful thought? When we are on our knees praying to our Father, we are adding to the bowls of incense. And not one prayer is ever lost. Acts 10:4 says, "And when he looked on him, he was afraid, and said, 'What is it, Lord?' And he said unto him, 'Thy prayers and thine alms are come up for a memorial before God.'"

Keeping a Prayer Journal

My friend Bill is in his eighties. He keeps a little notebook in his shirt pocket. If he's talking to someone and hears of a prayer need, he pulls that little notebook out of his pocket and writes it down. Once I mentioned to him that my mom was sick. He whipped his little book out and wrote her name down. Instead of just saying,

"I'll pray for her," he had action behind his words. And it made me feel good knowing my prayer was in his notebook and he would see it and pray over it.

I could kick myself for not keeping a journal earlier in my prayer life. It's wonderful to see all the prayers God has answered.

> I will remember the deeds of the Lord; yes, I will remember your miracles of long ago. I will consider all your works and meditate on all your mighty deeds. (Psalm 77:11–12)

For me, keeping a prayer journal is like a diary of prayers. It is a tribute to how wonderful God has been to me and my family. There's so much that happens in a day, week, month, or lifetime that we can't remember it all and it's easy to forget God's kindness and loyalty. We forget everything God has done and all of his awesomeness. We forget how He delivered us. My prayer journal serves as a reminder and a faith strengthener when I'm facing new trials. It helps me remember who He is: slow to anger and abounding in love. When we remember all He has done, we can keep walking in the right direction. These are the benefits of following God. And these are the benefits of keeping a prayer journal, so we never forget how He heals, forgives, satisfies, redeems, crowns, and answers prayers.

There was a prayer journal of sorts all the way back in the Old Testament. When Joshua and the Israelites were done wandering the desert, God caused the Jordan River to divide so they could cross over. He then had men from each tribe pick up a river stone to remember all that God had done during their journey.

Keeping a prayer journal is the same kind of memorial to God as that stone. Here are some suggestions.

1. Get a journal. Any journal will do. I usually get mine from TJ Maxx. Make sure you get one that has a good number of pages so it will last you awhile.
2. Write an entry and make sure you date it. Write it like you are talking right to God.
3. When a prayer is answered, put the date that God did it next to that prayer.
4. Go back and read it periodically, like monthly or quarterly. For me this is the fun part because I *love* to see how God has answered my prayers.

There are some mornings when I don't know what to pray for or how to pray. That's okay. Romans 8:26 says, "Likewise the Spirit also helpeth our infirmities: for we know not what we should pray for as we ought: but the Spirit itself maketh intercession for us with groanings which cannot be uttered."

What does that mean? Charles Ellicott's explanation in Ellicott's Bible Commentary for Romans 8:26 says, "When the Christian's prayers are too deep and too intense for words, when they are rather a sigh heaved from the heart than any formal utterance, then we may know that they are prompted by the Spirit Himself. It is He who is praying to God for us."[4]

When someone asked preacher and author Frances Chan, "What can I do to improve my prayer life?", he answered, "Be humble. Seek humility. Humble yourself." He went on to say, "We must come humbly before God's throne. Just think to yourself, 'Are you kidding me that I get to do this right now? Unreal. I'm about to come before God in prayer!'"[5]

Sometimes when we pray, we pray so small when our God is *so big*! What I mean is that we should go for the gusto when we're praying. God said He can move mountains for someone with the faith of a mustard seed.

> "For truly, I say to you, if you have faith like
> a grain of mustard seed, you will say to this
> mountain, 'Move from here to there,' and it will
> move, and nothing will be impossible for you."
> (Matthew 17:20)

Mustard seeds are usually about one to two millimeters in size—extremely small, like 1/64 of an inch. And I believe Jesus is saying that even though the mustard seed is so small, it actually grows into a twenty-foot-tall by twenty-foot-wide tree, not a tiny plant like many believe. Jesus's point is that it only takes a tiny amount of faith to "move mountains." "According to your faith let it be done to you" (Matthew 9:29). That's why only a tiny bit of faith can go a long, long way—even if it's 1/64 of an inch.

Have you heard the saying, "Go big or go home?" We have a big God, so why not pray big? God wants His people to take ownership of the blessings He has promised us.

> "The Lord will open to you his good treasury,
> the heavens, to give the rain to your land in its
> season and to bless all the work of your hands.
> And you shall lend to many nations, but you shall
> not borrow." (Deuteronomy 28:12)

My friend Beth was selling her house. She was a single mom to two children and wanted to move into a new townhouse where everything was new and fixed and working. We prayed with her at church, in our Bible study group, and at our mission meetings: "Lord, please sell Beth's house." But we were praying so teeny tiny to our big God, who had astonishing plans in store. Not only did Beth's house sell for the full asking price, but the people who bought it asked her to stay on rent-free to housesit for eighteen months! And here we were asking God to "just sell the house."

> "No eye has seen, no ear has heard, no heart has imagined, what God has prepared for those who love Him." (1 Corinthians 2:9)

One of the greatest testimonies of what prayer can do is the Brooklyn Tabernacle. The pastor, Jim Cymbala, didn't go to Bible college or seminary. Yet God called him to lead that church in the 1970s. His wife Carol is the choir director for their six-time Grammy Award-winning choir. She doesn't know how to read music, so she figures out the songs in her head and teaches the group by rote. By some standards, they may not seem qualified to lead a church, yet God called them to this ministry. And to what do they attribute their success? Their Tuesday night prayer meetings. Cymbala says it is the barometer of their church.

> If we call upon the Lord, He has promised in his Word to answer, to bring the unsaved to himself, to pour out his Spirit among us. If we don't call upon the Lord, He has promised nothing— nothing at all. It's as simple as that. No matter what I preach or what we claim to believe in our heads, the future will depend upon our times of prayer. [6]

It all begins and ends with prayer. After my divorce, praying the prayer of all prayers changed my life. I am living proof of unbelievable, answered prayer. Being able to go before the throne to our Father is an honor. I've learned that instead of focusing on myself, I must focus on God's mission for me. Through prayer, I have found hope.

My prayer journal

3

JOY IN FAMILY

I'M EXCITED TO write this chapter because I love my family. They're the best. They make me laugh and they make me proud. There have been times where they have made me cry. My kids and I, through God's grace, have been through a lot together. We have had our share of bumps and bruises, highs and lows, mountains and valleys. But through it all, God has sustained us.

Being a single parent isn't easy, that's for sure. There may be days when you're ready to throw in the towel. When you are the maid, cook, Uber driver, homework tutor, and sibling mediator, you may feel like you're walking through a minefield and there could be an explosion any minute. You may think, *How in the world will I navigate this on my own?*

Early after my divorce, I was at dinner with my friend Mary Kate, who nonchalantly mentioned Isaiah 54:5. "You know, the verse that says God is your Husband." What?? How had I never heard about this verse before? I ran home, tore open my Bible, and read this verse over and over until it was memorized in my heart and in my head.

> For thy Maker is thine husband; the LORD of hosts is his name; and thy Redeemer the Holy One of Israel; The God of the whole earth shall he be called.

God could be my Husband? But how? I was intrigued and excited at the thought. I wanted to know Him in this most intimate of ways. As I contemplated this verse, my heart saw how God could be even *better* than a husband.

1. **God is always there**. 100 percent of the time. He's never out of town, or preoccupied, or sick, or tired. He never leaves me. Hebrews 13:5b says, "For he hath said, 'I will never leave thee, nor forsake thee.'"
2. **God encourages me**. He told me I can do it all. I can handle anything. Philippians 4:13 says, "I can do all things through Christ which strengthens me."
3. **God makes me feel special**. Just when I need it, He gives me a word from Scripture that speaks to my heart. Or a rainbow in the sky that reminds me of his faithfulness. Or a hug from my child when I feel lonely. 1 Peter 2:9 states, "But ye are a chosen generation, a royal priesthood, an holy nation, a peculiar people; that ye should shew forth the praises of him who hath called you out of darkness into his marvelous light."

As I started to apply this concept to my life in the days, weeks, months ahead, it was comforting. I loved having God as my Husband. He was the first one I told if I had a tricky day with a student. He was the first one I talked to if I needed to discipline my child. I could sit in His presence and be real with Him. I could listen to Him while He made Himself known to me.

Having God as my Husband began a love relationship like I had never experienced before. Every day, I fell further in love with my Maker. As I studied the Bible more and more, I grew to love Jesus in such a powerful way. How can you not love someone who heals a blind man, cures a leper, restores a paralytic, brings back to life a widow's son, and feeds a multitude?

More importantly, how can you not love someone who died for you? Not just any death, but an agonizing, dreadful death. If you meditate on that and it doesn't melt your heart and make you crave a loving relationship with Him, what will?

You can't love anyone without knowing that person intimately and entirely. Do you know our Savior that way? If not, stop this second and pray for that kind of relationship.

Having God as my Husband was a gift to my children as well. They saw the joy in my life, and that gave them comfort. I never wanted them to be burdened with my aloneness. I never wanted them to feel that my happiness depended on them.

So that raises the question of what kind of single parent I wanted to be. What did I want my kids to see in me? For me, that was an easy answer. If we're to be imitators of Christ, I knew how I wanted to live my life.

- **Pure**. There you have it, plain and simple. My kids were not going to see a revolving door of men in my life. Despite an unsaved relative telling me to "Go buy some dating clothes and head to the corner beach bar," I had no intention of doing that. When I gave my life to the Lord, I trusted him in this area 100 percent. Maybe being single is what God had planned for my life, and I was okay with that. Finding another man was never my goal; serving the Lord was. In our journeys as single parents, we have to anchor our hearts and lives in God's truth and be proactive in pursuing it. If my children saw me content in my singleness, then they knew they could be also. And it wasn't just my kids who were watching—the world was. Living in purity in this world makes us stand out, and that gives glory to God.

- **Joyful**. I wanted to be a happy mom for my children. I wanted to be silly and light-hearted with them. I wanted to play hide-and-go-seek with them in the house. I wanted to eat pancakes for dinner. Yes, there were days I was stressed out and worried about paying the bills. But they didn't need to know that. Yes, there were days I was tired and all I wanted to do was take a nap—and sometimes I did, and that's okay too. Through all my emotions, I never wanted my kids to feel that my happiness depended on them, because it didn't.

- **Loving**. Because I love God with all my heart, it's easy to love my children unconditionally. Even when they disobey, my love will never backslide. Because I love my children, I will discipline them. The two go hand in hand—love and discipline. Just as God loves us and disciplines us, so should we do so with our children. Hebrews 12:5–6 tells us, "And ye have forgotten the exhortation which speaketh unto you as unto children, 'My son, despise not thou the chastening of the Lord, nor faint when thou art rebuked of him: For whom the Lord loveth he chasteneth, and scourgeth every son whom he receiveth.'" I love that—who the Lord *loves* He *disciplines*.

- **Organized**. It's hard to have joy in your home when things are always chaotic and disorganized. Kids thrive on structure, and so do I. I can't go to sleep at night unless I know everyone and everything around me is taken care of. If you are a single mom, it all falls on you.

Proverbs 31:27 tells us, "She watches over the affairs of her household and does not eat the bread of idleness."

- **Teacher of God's Word**. Most importantly, teach your children about Jesus. It's a sad home where the Bible doesn't get opened and used. Read Scripture to them, help them memorize verses, have family devotions, go to church, pray with them. Deuteronomy 6:7 instructs us, "And thou shalt teach them diligently unto thy children, and shalt talk of them when thou sittest in thine house, and when thou walkest by the way, and when thou liest down, and when thou risest up." Our kids are on loan to us from God. We're responsible for investing in their future and stewarding over them. We want them to be equipped to understand the Gospel and follow Jesus on their own someday.

During this season as a single parent, I had to be diligent and resistant to laziness or slothfulness. Don't get me wrong—I took the occasional nap, but only if my house was in order. My chief concern wasn't the perfect home, but rather a healthy home full of love, laughter, and order. I tried to keep my home free from physical and emotional clutter. These are some tips I learned as a single mom.

1. **Start your day off in prayer.** Ask the Lord for discernment on what is important and what is not.
2. **Don't put things off.** Things you can get done today, do them. If you let one thing pile up, four other items are right behind it ready to add to the pile. When the mail comes in, open it, discard it, or file it. If a permission slip comes home, sign it, put it back in your child's folder, and mark it on your calendar.
3. **Learn to say no**. It's okay. You can't commit to everything. Only commit to God. There are not enough

hours in the day to volunteer nonstop, especially when you are working and taking care of your children. Find other ways to spend quality time with them.

4. **Give the kids chores.** This was hard for me to do because I love to do everything myself in a particular way. But chores are good for the kids: they love to help, and chores teach them strong work ethics. Feeding the pets, making their beds, unloading the dishwasher, and folding the laundry are great ways to start your child off doing chores.

5. **Find rest for yourself.** I always give myself seven to eight hours of sleep. I can't function without a good night's sleep. And if I can't function, how can I take care of my children the way I want? After putting your children to bed, enjoy alone time, whether it be watching your favorite show, taking a candlelit bath, or reading a new novel. Find something that nourishes your soul and enjoy it.

Having Fun with Your Kids

Andrew Carnegie said, "There is little success if there is little laughter," and I agree with him. Laughter improves emotional health by releasing dopamine, which enhances the experience of pleasure. It also releases serotonin, which lifts your mood, and endorphins, which regulate pain and stress and induce euphoria.

So how do you bring laughter into your home? As single parents, our humor may abandon us when we're under stress. But it's important to look at the light side of things—and with God in control, there is always light.

Plan fun activities with your children. Even though single parent budgets are tight, there are tons of fun things to do that are free or inexpensive.

- Movie and popcorn night at home
- Swimming at a beach, lake, or city pool
- Fishing at a nearby lake or ocean
- Workshops at Home Depot
- Barnes and Noble: Mom gets a coffee, kids get a cookie. You both get a stack of magazines or books.
- Hiking the local trails
- Bike riding through your neighborhood
- Geocaching
- Planting a garden
- Strolling through a farmer's market
- Window shopping at the mall
- Touring a fire station
- Visiting the zoo
- Perusing the dollar store
- Crafting at home
- Camping in your backyard

One of my heart's desires was that my children would be well-travelled. But how do you travel on a single mom's budget? Be creative. What resources do you have?

One day I was watching the movie *The Holiday* with a girlfriend. If you haven't seen it, the characters played by Cameron Diaz and Kate Winslet live in different countries, they exchange homes, and vacation in the other's residence. It got me thinking: do people really do this? I Googled it and saw that yes, in fact, this is a real thing. There is a small annual fee, it's very safe, and there are unlimited possibilities.

The kids and I lived in a small beach house near the Gulf of Mexico in Florida. After praying about it, I listed our home on HomeExchange.com and immediately got multiple offers for home exchanges. Over the next few years, we swapped houses in a palatial home in Atlanta, a 100 year-old Victorian in Savannah, Georgia, and a 100 acre cattle ranch in Sparta, Tennessee. We celebrated the Fourth of July at a home in Washington, DC, watched the New Year's Eve ball drop in an apartment in New York City, and had an entire bed and breakfast to ourselves in Stafford Springs, Connecticut. What a blessing from God these trips were. They were wonderful vacations on an easy budget.

During another unforgettable summer, we took a 3,000 mile road trip, stopping at family members' homes along the way. We were gone three weeks and never had to stay in a hotel one night thanks to the invitations of sweet relatives.

These trips were monumental to us on our journey as a family. We bonded and connected during our time away together. We laughed until our stomachs hurt, and that's a good thing

- While I drove, the kids pulled feathers out of a pillow and put them on a sleeping head, so when the sleeper woke up, feathers floated around the person.
- We caught lightning bugs and used them as a nightlight while we slept—God's flashlight.
- We fed apples to the wild horses on the Appalachian Trail.
- We ate lunch at the *Seinfeld* Monk's Café.
- We took pictures in front of the gates of Graceland.
- We sampled 100 different sodas from around the world at the World of Coca-Cola.

I could go on and on. The point is that memories were made and hearts were happy.

Travelling Apps

There are some amazing websites out there that can aide single parents and make travelling easier. Here are a few.

- **TripHobo** features a selection of pre-planned itineraries to help busy would-be travelers choose their destinations and activities. Users can add their own activities to suit their preferences. The app's hotel suggestions and comparisons make booking accommodation a breeze.
- **TripIt** automates trip organizing by gathering confirmation emails to generate a master itinerary you can access from a smartphone, even offline.
- **TripCase** helps travelers automatically create itineraries based on confirmation emails they receive; displays a trip news feed with timely information and updates relevant to each segment of the trip.[7]

Although travelling alone with children can seem daunting and overwhelming, God will plan your steps. Isaiah 30:21 is so awesome: "And thine ears shall hear a word behind thee, saying, 'This is the way, walk ye in it, when ye turn to the right hand, and when ye turn to the left.'"

New Traditions

Even though your family may look different after a divorce, that doesn't mean you have to stop making memories. It's also important to create and continue your own family traditions and rituals. Traditions tell a story about a family and instill confidence in a child. They also strengthen the family bond, offer security to family members, and add to the seasonality of life. By doing this, we become connected with our kids. Some things we implemented and strengthened after the divorce were:

> **Devotions**. Each night, one child leads a devotion. It can be as long or as short as the child

wants. Sometimes it's just a prayer. Whatever God lays on that child's heart, we join in.

Thanksgiving. Before our meal, we have a scavenger hunt in the neighborhood. We break into two teams, and whichever team finishes the list first, *wins*. Items on our list have included a Slurpee cup from 7-11, a selfie in front of a landmark, or a shell from the beach, to name just a few. We also started to incorporate new dishes on our Thanksgiving menu: mac and cheese, fruit pie, sausage stuffing—a little bit of new along with a lot of the old too.

Christmas. There are so many opportunities this time of year. One the kids and I started volunteering for was setting up luminaries in our neighborhood on Christmas Eve. The neighbors loved them and so did we. Another one was on Christmas Day, we started a tradition of playing hot potato with a few presents that I bought, in addition to their other gifts. The kids love playing. Also we wear Christmas hats, and set an alarm for every fifteen minutes to swap. Gingerbread house-making competitions are a huge hit and get fairly heated.

Dinner Out. One night a week, someone picks a restaurant to eat at. There are lots of restaurants that offer free kid's meals, and we take advantage of those. A few are Applebee's, Bob Evans, Cody's Steakhouse, and Moe's.

Whatever you do to make your home joyful and memorable with your children, the bottom line is to give your child your attention. Put down your cell phone, your dish towel, and your calendar, and just be silly and spontaneous. And with God as your husband, you can enjoy the deepest level of intimacy and affection that you will ever know.

> Then was our mouth filled with *laughter*, and our tongue with singing: then said they among the heathen, The Lord hath done great things for them. (Psalm 126:2; emphasis added)

Be Careful

Now is a good time to bring up a very important matter. Who are we actually worshipping as single parents: our children or Jesus Christ? I had to examine my own heart about this after my divorce. Feeling that I had failed at marriage made me overcompensate by trying to be a successful mother in the world's eyes. I thought, *My kids may have divorced parents, but they will have the best grades, be the best at sports, and have the most friends.* I began to elevate my children to a state of perfection. When I saw what I was doing, I had to stop and remind myself that I don't serve the idol of my children. I serve a resurrected Jesus Christ and He alone reigns on the throne of my heart. He is the object of my worship. I knew I needed to be more honoring of God, and less absorbed by my children.

Our identity is as a child of God, not as a parent.

At the end of a busy day of being Mom, we should remind ourselves that God has called us to train our children in the way they should go (Proverbs 22:6). Passing on the legacy of our faith couldn't be a more significant calling. The Great Commission includes our homes with our kids. Embrace your role without grumbling, and God promises that as we shine our light into our homes, we will know that our labor was not in vain (Philippians 2:12–16).

Traveling with the kids

4

JOY IN CHURCH

WHEN I COME home from work, or a long day of running errands, the first thing I do is kick my shoes off. For me, it's the ultimate in relaxing. My heart sings, "I'm barefoot and I'm free!"

The same thing happens when I walk into church. No, I don't kick my shoes off. But I feel like I'm home. I'm relaxed and I'm free. These are my people. This is my tribe.

Sound silly? If you attend a church that makes your soul sing, you'll know what I'm talking about. It's just like having a good meal at a restaurant—you feel relaxed and well fed. The same thing happens to me after my pastor's sermon—I feel spiritually relaxed and well fed.

Don't get me wrong: there are times after my pastor's sermons when I feel the Holy Spirit pricking my heart, telling me I need to work on something. I don't necessarily feel relaxed, but I feel spurred to make changes in my life, whether it be with God, my kids, or my class.

God wants us in church. Why? Because being involved in church nurtures God's desire for us that we don't travel this journey alone. He wants us to grow and edify one another.

Hebrews 10:23–25 teaches us,

> Let us hold fast the profession of our faith without wavering; for he is faithful that promised; And let us consider one another to provoke unto love and to good works. Not forsaking the assembling of ourselves together, as the manner of some is; but exhorting one another: and so much the more, as ye see the day approaching.

God wants us to attend church to learn more about Him, draw closer to Him, and enjoy fellowship with other believers.

I had been attending a church for about ten years when the Holy Spirit started working on me. As I sat in the pew one Sunday after my divorce, I realized I was the only divorcee in there, and it made me feel very self-conscious. I felt like the third wheel at every potluck. And just like God does, he put another mom in my life at this time and we became fast friends. She invited me to her church, and the second I walked in, I knew this was where I was meant to "sharpen my iron."

I love the verse Proverbs 27:17: "Iron sharpeneth iron; so a man sharpeneth the countenance of his friend." This is an interesting vision of accountability. In Old Testament times, one iron blade was used to sharpen another blade until both became more effective tools. This visual aid of a common implement of work or war provides a practical model for many human relationships.[8]

Integrating this "sharpening iron" tool into my new life was instrumental to my effectiveness as a never-stop-growing Christian. My new pastor and fellow parishioners helped draw out the strengths and interests in my life. Thanks to my new church, I learned how to use the tools for what God had in place for me—in my work, in my ministry, and in my relationships.

Listen to what Charles Stanley says about church:

> God knows how important it is for us to have fellowship and to grow closer to Him by learning more about Him. Believers meet together, not to sit in pews and show off their best outfits, but so that through worship, Bible study, and prayer Christ may become more real and powerful in each person's life. Believers meet together to remind each other that God is faithful, and that His people are to be faithful, too.[9]

God doesn't want us to be alone. At each step of the way when God created the world, he pronounced that everything was "good." But then once he created Adam, a statement startles us: something is *not* good. "It is not good that the man should be alone" (Gen. 2:18). This was before the fall—before sin had entered the world. Adam was not yet complete; he needed community.

What does this show us? Although our deepest problems are sin and idolatry, our first problem was social isolation. Therefore, even today, in a world filled with society, Proverbs warns that the one who "isolates himself...breaks out against all sound judgment" (Proverbs 18:1). So God doesn't want us alone. He wants us surrounded in fellowship with other believers.

Finding a Home Church

Are you looking for a church? If you already have one, ask yourself if it's healthy and effective. Finding a church should begin with *prayer*. Ask God for discernment. Have Him lead your steps.

Take these items into consideration when choosing a church:

1. The first area of concern is doctrinal. What is the church teaching? There are eight doctrines of the church that are indispensable when seeking a fellowship that is teaching the truth.

   - **The Bible**—Does the church teach that the Bible is the Word of God? Second Timothy 3:16 teaches, "All Scripture is inspired by God and profitable for teaching, for reproof, for correction, for training in righteousness." Does the church advocate this doctrine?

   - **The Deity of Christ**—Does the church teach that Jesus Christ is not only the Son of God, but that He is God?

   - **The Virgin Birth of Jesus Christ**—Does the church teach that the Holy Spirit placed Him in the womb of the Virgin Mary?

   - **The Bodily Resurrection of Christ**—Does the church teach that Jesus fully conquered death and did all He said He would do, rising on the third day after His crucifixion?

   - **The Second Coming**—Does the church teach that Jesus is coming again?

   - **The Judgment**—Does the church teach that there is a time for each person to stand before almighty God and give an account for his or her life?

   - **Heaven and Hell**—Does the church teach that Christ's judgment will result in different eternal destinations for people?

   - **Salvation**—Does the church teach that Jesus Christ, the Son of God, went to the cross and died a sacrificial, atoning death, and that His sacrifice is the only avenue of salvation?

2. The next area of concern in finding a church is examining whether or not the church is building your

faith and discipling you. Is the church strengthening your relationship with God? Is the church enabling you to understand Scripture, and teaching you scriptural principles for living? Does is provide areas in which to serve?

3. The last area is discovering if the church has a ministry to the world. Is the church concerned about people around the world who have never heard the gospel? Is it evangelistic and missions-minded? Is it making an impact in its community and globally?[10]

Church membership was essential for me as a growing Christian. It increased my love for Christ and for God's people. My pastor taught me more about Jesus and how to serve Him with my life in new and wonderful ways that gave God honor and glory.

How to Connect at Church

Deep down, we all desire a real form of connection. We want people to know and accept us. Here are three important reasons to look to our church family for connection.

1. **You learn more about God when you connect with others at church.**

    Sitting in a circle with other Christians sharing your life story helps strengthen your own faith and you will walk away feeling encouraged or inspired. That's because God designed us to spur each other on in our faith.

    "And let us consider one another to provoke unto love and to good work. Not forsaking the assembling of ourselves together, as the manner

41

of some is; but exhorting one another: and so much the more, as ye see the day approaching." (Hebrews 10:24–25)

2. **You learn more about yourself when you connect with others at church.**

Allowing others to speak into your life helps you gain insight into who you are. My church family has seen things in me, good and bad, that I couldn't see. When you open yourself up to others, you allow light to shine in some dark places.

Sometimes we need reassurance, guidance, knowledge, or direction. God knew that finding connection with other Christians is the path for those occurrences.

3. **You realize you are not alone when you connect with others at church.**

Sometimes the two most powerful words in the English language are, "I understand." Sometimes you can breathe a sigh of relief when someone else says he or she has been through that exact same thing. Connection is powerful. It has the power to pull someone out of the darkness of isolation. "Blessed be God, even the Father of our Lord Jesus Christ, the Father of mercies, and the God of all comfort; Who comforteth us in all our tribulation, that we may be able to comfort them which are in any trouble, by the comfort wherewith we ourselves are comforted of God"(2 Corinthians 1:3–4).

4. **God never intended for us to do life alone.** Relationships with other Christians in an authentic

community reveals the power of the Holy Spirit by knitting us together.[11]

At my new church, we were encouraged to choose a home fellowship group from eight different ones. These home groups met once a week at a member's home. We prepared and ate dinner together, read through the Bible, often had the Lord's Supper. We prayed for and with each other. More often than not, our children would come also. My youngest son got his love for sloppy joes from eating them with our group.

Not only were we learning more about God, we were learning more about each other and becoming a tight-knit group. If someone lost a job, we would take up a collection for that person. If someone was going through a difficult parenting moment, we would talk it through. The ages in our group were varied, so a young parent could get godly advice from an older parent who had already gone through a similar situation in raising his or her children.

God wants us to enjoy fellowship with other believers. When I read in the Bible how the early church in Acts enjoyed fellowship, I want this for myself.

> And they continued steadfastly in the apostles' doctrine and fellowship, and in breaking of bread, and in prayers. (Acts 2:42)

We can break it down like this

1. "And they continued steadfastly…" They had an earnest desire for more knowledge.
2. "In the apostles' doctrine and fellowship…" They were eager to hear what the apostles had to share about our Savior

3. "And in breaking of bread..." They enjoyed the Lord's Supper together.
4. "And in prayers." No doubt they prayed for each other and for the Kingdom.

Continuing in Acts 4:32–35, we read,

> Now the multitude of those who believed were of one heart and one soul; neither did anyone say that any of the things he possessed was his own, but they had all things in common. And with great power the apostles gave witness to the resurrection of the Lord Jesus. And great grace was upon them all. Nor was there anyone among them who lacked; for all who were possessors of lands or houses sold them, and brought the proceeds of the things that were sold, and laid them at the apostles' feet; and they distributed to each as anyone had need.

Just wow! That's all I can say. What a beautiful picture, isn't it? Don't you want that for yourself? Let's dig deeper into this.

The first sentence sets the tone for what follows: "All the believers were one in heart and mind." Luke is describing the extraordinary sense of unity that the early believers felt. The phrase "heart and mind" indicates that they were more than just in intellectual agreement. They were united in their faith. They deeply experienced the feeling of a common bond in Christ.

The experience was so intense that it spilled over into the practical issue of possessions: "No one claimed that any of his possessions was his own, but they shared everything they had."[12]

It's important to note that the sharing of possessions was not a *rule*, but an *attitude* of all believers. A mature believer is attentive to the needs of the church family. And that's how I felt with my church family—they were attentive to my needs.

One night I got a call from my pastor. "Jack and I are coming over with a rotisserie chicken and baked potatoes!" These two men, my pastor and my deacon, knew that a cooked dinner for my kids and me would be a blessing—and it was. After we ate, we sat in the backyard and talked about whatever was on our hearts. I'll never forget that night, and how these two busy men took time out of their day to bless a single mom.

Another time, my church organized a yard clean-up at my house. Eight people from church gave up their Saturday morning to cut limbs and pull weeds in my yard…in June…in Florida. We had a pile of trimmings so large it took three truckloads to get it all to the dump.

I certainly wasn't looking for a handout from church, and I don't believe I ever asked for help of any kind. But the closeness I shared with my pastor and church family punctured their hearts to be Christ-like. They wanted to help their sister in Christ. Their help was appreciated and needed, and receiving a blessing from them touched my heart.

There was something bigger going on that I was a part of. My church family was following Jesus's example of servanthood. Even though Jesus was widely popular, He never sought prestige or power. He came into this world as a servant and that was His number one commitment.

Jesus's example of servanthood calls on us to treat others how we should be treated. His example releases the love of God in our lives and enables us to make a difference.

Watching our church in action was wonderful for my children to witness. They saw Christians walking the walk and not just talking the talk. Our church family was not selfish. They humbly and sacrificially served us.

The Bible tells us, "As we have opportunity, let us do good to all people" (Galatians 6:10).

Do you want to feel closer to others in your congregation? Then give of yourself in whatever way you can. As a single parent, money is tight, but how about giving hospitality? Invite people over to your home or out for coffee. Give a fellow mom a morning out. Give a child in the nursery some attention. You will see a bond form out of this closeness.

I couldn't have stayed the course without the church family God put in my life. They pushed me, pulled me, and grew with me. If I hadn't gotten involved in church, if I had hid in the back and snuck out during the closing prayer, I would have missed out on huge blessings from God.

Rubbing shoulders with God's family has given me a lifetime of memories. I have collected experiences by following Jesus *with* my church. It's a beautiful thing, isn't it? God's people are brought into bonds of friendships in the church.

Church is a refuge

5

MY DAD USED to say, "Have the kind of friend that will bail you out of jail in the middle of the night!" Thankfully I never had to be bailed out of jail, but I do have friends I would call if I ever needed to.

My deepest friendships are the ones that have been with me through life's soul-shaking changes. Like Clint Eastwood, they've seen the good, the bad, and the ugly. They made space for me when life was shaky. And they rejoiced with me when all was well. When my oldest son was having teen angst, they were there. When I won Teacher of the Year through our city association at my school, they were there. We've cried and celebrated together.

There is something very special about a Christian friendship. When two people are devoted to Jesus, that spiritual unity forms a camaraderie that is treasurable. Not only are they our friends, but they are our brothers and sisters in Christ.

**Have the kind of friendships that will encourage
and challenge you in your walk with Christ.**

There have been times when my friend Rory has come to me and said, "You need to pick up the pace." If I am being lazy in my walk with the Lord, she is quick to point it out. I appreciate that, and I'm not offended. A good friend is one who points us to Christ, not to the world. That friend will stand side by side with you, pointing you to the Gospel truth. It's okay to give friends criticism if it's scriptural, and is done lovingly and constructively.

Even Jesus said in John 8:11, "'Go and sin no more.'" He wasn't offending or degrading. He gave a simple admonishment, an encouragement to live differently. He was not afraid of pointing out the best way to live.

Sometimes, our pastor will tell us something in his sermon that is difficult to hear, and he always follows it with, "I tell you this because *I love you*." It is not loving to allow a professing Christian to continue in a sin that will bring God's consequences upon the person, his or her family, or his or her church. Jesus gave clear instructions for handling situations in which a brother or sister is caught up in a sin: "'If your brother or sister sins, go and point out their fault, just between the two of you. If they listen to you, you have won them over'" (Matthew 18:15). Good friends will do this. And good friends will take their advice.

God Gives Us Our Friends

I agree with Ralph Waldo Emerson when he said, "I didn't FIND my friends. The good Lord gave them to me."

God puts people in our lives to enrich us, challenge us, and encourage us. After my divorce, there were friends I stayed in touch with. But slowly, God started putting new friendships in my life. I trusted Him that He had a new and perfect plan for me. He has created us in a way that we need friendships and He will provide the right ones. Sometimes it may not be when we want it or how we want it, but don't worry. He will provide the right person in His timing.

I've never heard someone say, "I wish I had less friends." That would be silly, wouldn't it? When my kids were in elementary school and learning to navigate friendships, I always told them, "To *have* a friend you need to *be* a friend." It sounds too simple but it's true. Someone has to take the initiative. Sometimes friendships are hard work, but they're worth it. Staying in touch by making a phone call or grabbing a cup of coffee takes time out of our days, but it's so important to keep that lifeline going.

The Bible makes it clear: we need friends to inspire, encourage, challenge, and love us—and your friends need you too.

Say what you will about social media, but I love it. Used in the right way, Facebook and Instagram are great opportunities to stay in touch with friends. I love seeing pictures of their kids, their vacations, their holidays. Roughly two thirds of social media users say that staying in touch with current friends and family members is a major reason they use these sites, while half say that connecting with old friends they've lost touch with is a major reason behind their use of these technologies.[13]

Before social media, there was old-fashioned letter writing. In my teens, I remember writing furiously a couple times a week to my friend Lisa, who lived 1,100 miles away. We were great pen pals and loved to hear from each other. I would get a letter from her, and immediately sit down to write her back. We always had the prettiest stationary from Current, and a couple of hard-working pens. We rocked the post office with our correspondence.

These days, we shoot each other a text a couple times a month. Or we're the first to "like" each other's posts on Facebook. Whatever works to keep our friendship going, and it's acceptable to both parties, is okay.

Good friends will stop their lives to share in your good times. I have too many examples of this to list, but when my daughter was in kindergarten, she was chosen to speak at her school's banquet. The theme was "Who is your hero?" My heart burst when she said, "My mom." My friend Beth (also a single mom) raced from work right to the banquet so she could share that special moment with me. I'll never forget what my daughter said that night, and I'll never forget that Beth joined me to share the evening.

My life is so much richer and more blessed with the Christian friends God placed in my life. After my divorce, I needed a strong community of people I could count on if I needed help with my children, a good book to read, a stop-and-pray-with-me moment, or a minute to share some good news.

In Heaven, we will enjoy true friendship with all other believers. Our future is a world of friendship. I don't know about you, but I can't wait to worship in Heaven with my friends.

So what does the greatest friend of all say about friendships? Let's take a look.

> "Greater love hath no man than this, that a man lay down his life for his friends." (John 15:13)

> A man that hath friends must shew himself friendly: and there is a friend that sticketh closer than a brother. (Proverbs 18:24)

> A friend loveth at all times, and a brother is born for adversity. (Proverbs 17:17)

> Behold, how good and how pleasant it is for brethren to dwell together in unity. (Psalm 133:1)

> Beloved, let us love one another: for love is of God; and every one that loveth is born of God, and knoweth God. (1 John 4:7)

Multigenerational Friendships

Before I even knew there was a name for this, I was doing it. I am drawn to people of all age groups. I have friends who are twenty years younger than me, and friends who are twenty years older than me. It's always been a given in my life. I haven't purposely sought out that age difference, it's just come naturally. I am very thankful for these multigenerational friendships. I love hearing from my friend Toni about her children, who are ages nine, seven, five, and three. And on the flipside, my friend Rory shares her adventures about retirement. It sure keeps my life interesting. I need the insights shared with me from the younger generation as well as those more seasoned women in life. And I have found that hearts matter more than age.

I was in my early twenties when I had my first older, woman friend. Her name was Jean and she was in her sixties. Jean treated me like a peer instead of a mentee. We met at work, but our friendship grew outside of the workplace. We went shopping together, had lunch together, and sometimes I would go to her house. She would show me her old scrapbooks, and she and her husband would make dinner. Those were great times. My friendship with Jean was fun and natural and easy. There was no drama with her, like there was with my same-age friends. She gave stellar advice, had amazing stories, and wasn't judgmental. She also had a *joie de vivre* that was both engaging and inspiring to me as I tried to find my place in the world. And the fact that she was active in her church did not go unnoticed by me, who was a haphazard Christian at the time.

According to a study done by Barna, when asked if an individual had a friend from another generation, 72 percent of Christians said yes. By comparison, four in ten non-Christians (41 percent) lack friendships with anyone outside their age groups. Church attendance enhances this tie between faith and friendship; churched Americans are significantly more likely to have friends both old and young (32 percent versus 22 percent of unchurched). Churched adults confirm that these relationships are often made at their places of worship (44 percent of those with older friends, 32 percent of those with younger friends).[14]

Whatever the age difference, God wants us to have friends in our lives. Have you heard this saying before?

> You are the average of the five people you spend the most time with.

The Bible says the same thing.

> Do not be misled: "Bad company corrupts good character."(1 Corinthians 15:33)

> Walk with the wise and become wise, for a companion of fools suffers harm. (Proverbs 13:20)

Think about your friends. Are they solid Christians, completely dedicated to following God no matter what? Or are they lukewarm and half-hearted in their faith, if they even believe at all? No one is perfect, that's for sure. We all have room for improvement. In our friendships, we should be surrounding ourselves with strong Christians who love God and love their families and seek to better themselves every day.

Ways to Make Godly Friends

- Reach out to people at church, the gym, your child's school, your neighborhood
- Get involved at outreaches, volunteer activities, PTA, MOPS
- Organize a get-together, like a book club or a clothing swap

- Research online sites such as:
  - Hellomamas.com
  - The Mommies Network
  - Cafemom.com
  - Circle of Moms
  - Baby Center

Examples of Friendships in the Bible

If you have ever wondered what great friendships look like, the Bible gives us some amazing examples. A theme of friendship is woven throughout Scripture.

David and Jonathan

To me, this friendship stands out the most. I love how 1 Samuel 18:1–4 describes their friendship.

> And it came to pass, when he had made an end of speaking unto Saul, that the soul of Jonathan was knit with the soul of David, and Jonathan loved him as his own soul. And Saul took him that day, and would let him go no more home to his father's house. Then Jonathan and David made a covenant, because he loved him as his own soul. And Jonathan stripped himself of the robe that was upon him, and gave it to David, and his garments, even to his sword, and to his bow, and to his girdle.

This is a great example of male friendship lacking in our modern culture. Men don't often form such close bonds. Jonathan showed the true core of a great friendship, loving another as you love yourself. He was also sacrificial in his love for David, by giving him items that represented his power and position. This friendship was one of love and loyalty.

Elijah and Elisha

This honorable friendship showed the significance of wisely choosing friends. Elisha was so devoted to his friend and mentor Elijah that he declared in 2 Kings 2:2, "As the Lord liveth, and as thy soul liveth, I will not leave thee."

We tend to become like our peers, so it is important to choose friends who are knowledgeable, devout, and eager about what they do.

Moses and Aaron

A true partnership of two friends working together to do something great. Moses wasn't a good speaker, but Aaron was. By working together, they accomplished God's will.

Naomi and Ruth

No jokes about mothers-in-law here. Ruth refused to let Naomi be alone. She pledged her life to the destitute Naomi. In Ruth 1:16–17, Ruth tells Naomi,

> "Intreat me not to leave thee, or to return from following after thee: for whither thou goest, I will go; and where thou lodgest, I will lodge: thy people shall be my people, and thy God my God."

What an example of unconditional love and self-sacrifice.

Our Ultimate Friend is God

Think about your best, *best* friend. What are that person's qualities? What do you like about that person? You may say he or she is caring, easy to talk to, empathetic, kind, truthful, patient. Now multiply that times 1,000 and you have your ultimate friend, our Lord and Savior Jesus Christ.

I remember when I was in elementary school belting out the lyrics in chapel to "What A Friend We Have in Jesus," written by Joseph M. Scriven.

> What a friend we have in Jesus,
> All our sins and griefs to bear!
> What a privilege to carry
> Everything to God in prayer!

We were made for friendship with God. He doesn't just want us to know *about* him; He wants us to *know* Him. The Bible tells us to submit to Jesus as our King, trust Him as our Savior, value Him as our Treasure, and enjoy Him as our Friend. Is there anything that sounds more beautiful?

Jesus is our ultimate friend. Do you know of any other friend who will give you what you need even though it is going to cost the person something? And would that friend leave his or her home for you? Would that person be willing to leave a grand position to live in poverty and help you for the rest of his or her life? Would this person be willing to live an entire life for you, to that person's detriment, just for your future? Would the person be willing to be hounded, tortured, struck, whipped, and murdered for you so that you would have life eternal?

On the night before His death, Jesus gathered His disciples together one last time. He wanted to prepare them for the next day and everything afterward. In the middle of all this, He said, "'No longer do I call you servants, for the servant does not know what his master is doing; but I have called you friends, for all that I have heard from my Father I have made known to you'" (John 15:15). What an unbelievable honor! Jesus calls us friends! I don't even feel worthy of this title. If He hadn't said it Himself, I never could have given myself that label.

Charles Spurgeon describes Jesus on the cross as an act of friendship. He writes, "He looked down from the cross and saw all the people denying him and betraying him and forsaking him and mocking him and rejecting him and in the greatest act of friendship in the history of the world, he stayed."[15]

Jesus said, "'Greater love has no one than this, that someone lays down His life for a friend'" (John 15:13), and that is what our friend Jesus did on the cross. That's why the cross is the highest symbol of friendship. Everything else He did in His life and ministry was leading up to this one enormous action of self-sacrificing love. And because Jesus calls us His friends, He willingly laid down His life for us that we might live by confessing our sins and believing in Him as our Savior. It is at the cross that we see the immensity of His devotion to us.

Even though Jesus said we are His friends, we shouldn't be flippant about calling Him our buddy, chum, or pal. Our friendship with Him is not trivial. Jesus offers Himself to us as both our King and our Friend.

Doing this life with my friends has been a joy. After my divorce, they stuck closer than some family, and often knew me better. The friends God gave me often prayed bigger things for me than I prayed for myself. Most importantly, true friends remind you in every encounter who and what is most important. And I certainly couldn't have put one foot in front of the other without my Heavenly Friend.

With my friend, Doris.
Multigenerational friendships are the best.

6

JOY IN SERVICE

"THERE'S AN HOUR I will never get back," said no volunteer ever.

Embarrassing confession: there was a time when my heart wasn't convicted for missions. I felt that people in poor countries needed to "get their act together, 'cause we here in the United States can't take care of the whole world." Just typing that now makes me squirm because I see how shallow of a believer I used to be.

Thankfully, the Holy Spirit got a firm grasp on me and shook me into accepting the truth. I was sitting in church one Sunday, waiting for the service to start and reading our announcements and upcoming events that were flashing on the screen in front of me: Spaghetti Dinner...Beach Baptism...Peru Mission Trip. *Hmmm... Peru mission trip? That sounds exciting. Maybe I could go on that?*

But Satan was right on my shoulder, saying, "Nah, you don't have anything to offer. You can't pay for it. You don't have anyone to watch your children." Good old Satan, always ready to fill your head with doubt and lies. That's his number one weapon. Every lie has its source in him. It's his native language. His object is to kill, destroy, and murder, and his scheme is to lie. If he can get you to believe a lie, he will bind you with it. He certainly wanted to thwart all efforts of me serving the Lord on the mission field.

But God is more powerful than Satan and his lies. All through the sermon, I kept thinking and fidgeting about that trip. While the Holy Spirit was making internal transformations in me, external action was getting ready to happen. Frances Chan writes that the Spirit fuels us so powerfully from the inside that His active presence is tangible and indisputable. Once this internal change takes place, you can't help but take action.[16]

While sitting during that sermon, something was bubbling up inside of me and about to flood out. It was like I was Yellowstone National Park and the Holy Spirit was Old Faithful.

At the last "Amen," I couldn't get to the Peru Mission Trip sign-up table fast enough. By complete faith, I signed up to go on the mission trip right then and there. No, I didn't know how I was going to pay for it. And no, I didn't know who would watch my kids for nine days while I was gone. But I did know one thing: I felt such a strong swell of faith and desire overcome me that I *knew* this was what God was calling me to do. I was completely walking by faith and not by sight. If I had listened to the enemy, I would have missed out on some wonderful blessings God had in store for me.

Fast-forward nine months. Not only did I go to Peru, but my trip was completely funded by donations. I didn't have to pay a penny. My children's dad agreed to watch them while I was gone. God was already working all things out for my good. So off I went to Peru with eight other church members to labor with the indigenous. By working with local churches, we built houses, worked at a feeding center, and organized Vacation Bible School for the children.

Don't think for a second that I am patting myself on the back for any of this. God did it all. "The steps of a good man are ordered by the Lord" (Psalm 37:23).

Over the next several years, I served on multiple short-term mission trips, travelling to Lithuania, Latvia, England, Poland, Germany, Ukraine, Czech Republic, Columbia, Panama, and more. Each trip was fully funded by donations of people who believed in the work my church was doing. This was a miracle! One incident in particular stands out to me. My oldest son, Kyle, and I were leaving for Lithuania in a week, and we were still short over a thousand dollars for our trip. I was praying that God would provide the money. Miraculously, I got a phone call from my Elder saying that a local businessman had heard about our trip and wanted to make a donation for Kyle and me. The donation was more than we needed. It taught me that not only does God provide, but He gives us more than we need. When He sends, He also equips.

There is no way I would have been able to take these trips on a preschool teacher's salary with four children to support. And multiply those trips times two: after my first trip to Peru, I started taking one of my children with me on each trip. I wanted my kids to have an international perspective on doing God's work. I wanted them to develop a servant's heart, witness cultural differences, and learn the value of giving as they pour into the lives of others. They always returned home with a deeper sense of what it means to be blessed as they see the value in what they have and realize the world is bigger than their backyard. I wanted my kids to see that by helping others, they were allowing those people to encounter Jesus. They were being equipped to travel the path of God's Word. God allows us to be beacons of light by reaching others with the hope and truth found in His Word.

Each child also loved having Mom to himself or herself for a few weeks. Even though we were part of a team, my kids they felt like they had one-on-one time with Mom. We definitely were able to maximize our time together on these mission trips, and that strengthened our relationships.

Serving Others

God has called all of us to serve because it is through service that we are best able to demonstrate the love of Jesus. As Christ followers, Jesus gives us specific instructions on how to serve others. In Mark 10, He says that every day in our life we should put the interests of others before our own interests. We should always want to meet the needs of everyone else.

> "But it shall not be so among you. But whoever would be great among you must be your servant, and whoever would be first among you must be slave of all. For even the Son of Man came not to be served but to serve, and to give his life as a ransom for many." (Mark 10:43–45)

Jesus reminds us that He did not come to be served, but to serve. That is staggering. If anyone should be served, it is the Son of God, the Lord of Lords, and the King of Kings. Yet Jesus's life on earth was filled with examples of serving others. He never placed Himself in a position above others. He led by serving and He loved by serving. He washed feet. He fed thousands. He healed the sick. He spent time with people no one else wanted to be around.

To be followers of Christ, we should always be looking for ways to meet the needs of others. We should love others so radically that they wonder why. We can do this through our talents, abilities, and gifts. Our standard of life should be putting others first. We shouldn't be thinking about ourselves and our own desires, but what others don't have that we can give them To be a servant means we genuinely care about others.

Are you keeping your eyes, hearts, and schedules open for Holy Spirit-arranged meetings? Jesus was not stressed by time. He didn't care what others thought of Him. He didn't have a list of tasks to accomplish each day. He followed His promptings to love, help, and serve others. No task was below Him, and no person was unworthy. Jesus showed that serving and humility go hand in hand.

> Do nothing from selfish ambition or conceit, but in humility count others more significant than yourselves. Let each of you look not only to his own interests, but also to the interests of others. Have this mind among yourselves, which is yours in Christ Jesus. (Philippians 2:3–5)

Jesus served us to the point of giving His own life for our sins.

To be a servant, each of us must stop focusing on ourself and meet the needs of others. If we do this without expecting recognition from people, Scripture promises that God will honor us.

> "If any man serve me, let him follow me; and where I am, there shall also my servant be: if any man serve me, him will my Father honour." (John 12:26)

My friend Ron is one of the finest servants I know. Most of his life has been serving others, first our country for twenty-seven years in the Air Force, then twenty-five years in Christian education. Now he is retired, but don't let that fool you. He is still serving. His ministry, Helping Hands, goes into the community and provides assistance to others. He has aided a moving widow, performed yard work for a single mom, and cooked and delivered Thanksgiving dinners to shut-ins. His motto and life verse is "Standing in the Gap," which comes from Ezekiel 22:30a: "And I sought for a man among them who should build up the wall and stand in the breach before me for the land." Ron continues to serve because, as he says, "I enjoy doing things that nobody else wants to do. I don't need thanks or recognition; just knowing that I made a difference is enough. When my wife and I retired, we wanted to serve faithfully for the blessings from Jesus. Nothing else!" What a heart for serving the Lord.

We can't speak on servanthood without talking about Billy Graham, America's pastor and the world's most renowned evangelist. He brought millions to Christ through his international crusades. Without a doubt, when he died at the age of ninety-nine and entered Heaven, he heard God utter the words, "Well done, good and faithful servant." This phrase can be found in Matthew 25 in the parable of the talents, a story about servants entrusted with money. Those who multiplied their money or talents, much like Graham who spread God's message to millions, are celebrated by God. Billy Graham was the humblest of servants, once saying, "I despise all this attention on me...I'm not trying to bring people to myself, but I know that God has sent me out as a warrior."

Billy Graham was a simple milk farmer from North Carolina with a thick, Southern accent, and God used him to be a world changer. And isn't that the way of God? He takes regular, everyday people, like you and me, to do astonishing things. God did this all throughout the Bible.

- Noah was a drunk
- Abraham was too old
- Isaac was a daydreamer
- Jacob was a liar
- Leah was ugly
- Joseph was abused

- Moses had a stuttering problem
- Gideon was afraid
- Samson had long hair and was a womanizer
- Rahab was a prostitute
- Jeremiah was too young
- David was an adulterer *and* a murderer
- Elijah was suicidal
- Isaiah preached naked
- Jonah ran from God
- Naomi was a widow
- Job went bankrupt
- John the Baptist ate bugs
- Andrew lived in the shadow of his big brother
- Peter denied Christ
- All the disciples fell asleep while praying (and ran away when Jesus really needed them)
- Martha worried about everything
- The Samaritan woman was divorced (more than once)
- Mary Magdalene was demon-possessed
- Zaccheus was too small
- Timothy had an ulcer
- Paul was a Christian-killer
- Lazarus was dead[17]

So if you're thinking you have no talents or abilities to serve God, you're wrong. God can use you right where you are for His Kingdom. Pray about it. Keep your heart open to the Holy Spirit's leading.

One friend of mine who did just that was Marlene, who doesn't enjoy speaking in front of crowds. It's not her comfort zone. But the Holy Spirit directed her to lead a women's Bible study at her workplace. She was completely compelled to do this; the Holy Spirit flooded her and she couldn't *not* do it. She got the okay from her boss and did a great job leading the study.

What I love is that Marlene was faithful to respond to this call of ministry. You can't deny the power of the Holy Spirit when He has a forceful grip on you. May that kind of force be with all of us.

> For it is God who works in you, both to will and
> to work for his good pleasure. (Philippians 2:13)

When God calls you to do something, He will equip you. When He called Moses to lead the people of Israel, He didn't then say "good luck!" He gave Moses a helpmate in Aaron. He gave him a cool stick. He completely equipped him.

God Can Use You Right Where You Are

A few years back, I had a girl in my class we'll call P. She didn't like school, didn't seem to like me, and certainly didn't want her parents to leave her in my classroom. She would cry, kick, and hit at drop-off each morning. It got to the point that when I saw the door open and she was there, my whole body would tense up, like I was bracing for impact. The little thing would look like she just rolled out of bed: hair matted, eyes sleepy, clothes wrinkled. I knew that to make it through the year I needed God's help. I started praying for Him to give me strength. He spoke to my heart with these words.

> **Me**: Lord, I need Your help. I don't know what
> to do with P.
> **God**: Love her more.
> **Me**: Say what?
> **God**: Love her more.
> **Me**: But God, sometimes she's not lovable!
> **God**: Well sometimes, you're not either.

Whoa! Those God gotcha moments can be painful at times, can't they?

But I did what He said. I started loving P more. When she came in the door, I took her by the hand and pulled her on my lap and snuggled her. I got a hairbrush just for her and started brushing her hair. I started telling her multiple times during the day that I loved her, and that God did too. Guess what happened? She started walking into my classroom smiling, excited to see me. I would feel someone hugging my legs during the day, and I would look down and it was P. It turns out that her parents were getting divorced, she was bouncing between two homes, sometimes late at night, and her life was in disarray and chaos. But God is orderly and loving, and through Him, He used me to work in P's life.

I'm not trying to take any hero-credit here. I didn't do anything. God did it all. He spoke to me and I listened to His calling, although I was reluctant at first. But I tell this story to underline the fact that God can use you right where you are. He will *use* you and *equip* you. All you have to do is listen and obey.

There is a man in the Bible named Shamgar. He is only mentioned in one verse, but what a verse!

> After him was Shamgar the son of Anath, who
> killed 600 of the Philistines with an oxgoad, and
> he also saved Israel. (Judges 3:31)

600 Philistines! With an oxgoad! Not a sword or a spear, but an oxgoad, which is the jawbone of an ox. And he helped save Israel, which is a pretty big task. Shamgar accepted the challenge from God and used what he had—an oxgoad—right where he was. God used him and equipped him. And he got twenty-two words written about him in the Old Testament.

For me, that one short verse displays God's ability to do flabbergasting, staggering things in a person. And God wants to do astonishing things using you too.

Ways to Serve God

It's exciting to walk hand-in-hand with God serving others. I told you about my love for missions and how the Holy Spirit completely compelled me to serve on short-term mission trips. Where is the Holy Spirit directing you? Where is He calling you? Do you feel an urgency to help somewhere?

- Do you have a heart for the homeless and poor? Does your heart pound every time you drive by someone destitute and lacking? Homeless shelters and soup kitchens are always looking for volunteers and donations. My son, Kyle, has started a Cheeseburger Outreach, where he visits parks and distributes McDonald's cheeseburgers to the homeless. It also opens the door for him to share the Gospel and pray with them.
- Do you crave to help, protect, and enhance the lives of the unborn? Many pregnancy centers partner with committed individuals willing to donate of their time, collect donations, assist with mailings, or host a baby bottle boomerang.
- Do you have a soft spot for the elderly? Would you love to make someone's day by spending time with them? Nursing homes are always looking for helpers to lead a worship service, serve during meals, visit the elderly, or organize their library.

Read your church bulletin for upcoming outreaches or short-term mission trips. Ask for the

Holy Spirit's leading. He will direct your steps as you are walking with Him, and before you know it, you will be at the place He wants you. He has a perfect plan for your life and will guide you every step of the way to fulfill that plan. He already has something planned for you; all you have to do is wait for His timing.

If you are struggling with the thought of serving others, ask yourself why?

- Like me with missions, is it a heart issue? Ask God to alter it and stretch you. He will teach you to serve others with love and compassion.
- Is it a time concern? Do you have too much on your plate? Ask God to show you ways to free up your schedule.
- Do you help those around you? Let others get in line before you at the store. Help a struggling mom you see.
- Are you listening to God? He will make opportunities for you throughout your day. Follow his leading and prompting.
- Is your heart hurting from your divorce? Does the thought of helping others overwhelm you when you can barely help yourself? The simplest remedy for loneliness and depression is focusing on others who are hurting or in need.

Be ready for your heart to change and grow as you serve. This is because you are experiencing joy and peace from being obedient to God's calling. Your heart certainly changes when you see miracles happen in the lives of the ones you are serving. By developing the spiritual gifts God gave you, you are forming bonds by working alongside others. What a joy it is to experience God's presence in new ways. Ultimately God is not only working through you, but in you. *We* are the ones who are changing when we serve.

Peru Mission Trip

7

JOY IN WORK

AFTER SURRENDERING MY life to Christ after my divorce, the doors that continued to fly open were astonishing, and sometimes laughable in their magnitude. I couldn't have begun to imagine what God had in store for me. I couldn't have even prayed for the blessings God bestowed on me because they were beyond my dreams.

After my divorce I wanted, and needed, to line up a job. God knew my heart and knew I wanted to be on the same schedule as my children. When they were home, I wanted to be home. Working at their school was definitely on my radar, but I didn't have any feelers out yet. I was just waiting to see how God worked it out. I was definitely banking on Psalm 37:4–5: "Delight thyself also in the Lord and he shall give thee the desires of thine heart. Commit thy way unto the Lord; trust also in him; and he shall bring it to pass."

One day, a former teacher of my two oldest children came to me asking if I would be interested in working in preschool.

"The job is yours if you want it," she said. I hadn't told anyone my desire to work there. I had not even filled out an application. Yet here was God, handing me the job of my dreams: working at my children's school, being able to see them throughout the day, and being on the same schedule as them. He was working everything out for my good. My heart swelled with love for my Maker. He's so good to me!

If it is from Him, He makes the first move. He initiates. He opens the door.

Here was tangible proof of God's provision. This job offer wasn't coincidental or random. He rules over everything. Of Him, through Him, to Him.

> For of him, and through him, and to him, are
> all things: to whom be glory for ever. (Romans
> 11:36)

Thus began one of the biggest blessings of my life: my career as a preschool teacher. My children go to a Christian school, so not only was I around my kids, but I was surrounded by some of the strongest Christians I had ever met. God had me hedged in with co-workers who I could pray and worship with all the live long day. Talk about iron strengthening iron!

Some of my best friends to this day came from my job—not only co-workers but also parents of children in my class. You never know what God has in store when He opens a door. My dear friend Mary and I hit it off the year I taught her son Caleb. We became fast friends. I went on to teach her two other children, and it was no small blessing to teach my dear friend's children.

Working Out of Joy

God wants us to work. But He also wants us to work out of joy, not duty. We find this in 1 Peter 5:2: work "not because you must, but because you are willing, as God wants you to be; not pursuing dishonest gain, but eager to serve." This is the kind of God we have. He wants us to love what we do *and* do it with gusto—with our whole hearts.

> And whatsoever ye do, do it heartily, as to the Lord, and not unto men. (Colossians 3:23)

So whatever kind of work you're doing—sweeping, filing, fixing cars—do it heartily. Don't be lazy. Give it all you've got. Work like God is your boss because it brings glory to Him. Always remember that it is God for whom we work, not humans. If we view ourselves as servants, Christ is our true boss, so we should work diligently and with integrity.

And why should we do this? The next verse tells us.

> Knowing that from the Lord you will receive an inheritance as your reward. You are serving the Lord Christ. (Colossians 3:24)

The incentive comes from knowing there's a reward for those who serve Christ. Who doesn't want a reward from God? That's pretty good motivation for me.

Money should not be our motivation. Success should not be our motivation. Christ is our motivation. He gave us our employment. He wants us to do it heartily and He will reward us for it.

CAROL SCHREIBER

Every Job is a Ministry

Teaching preschool at a Christian school didn't bring a large paycheck, but it was a ministry. I was able to minister to the children in my class and also their parents. Truthfully, any job can be a ministry if you're showing the love of Christ to those around you. The word *ministry* comes from the Latin word *ministerium*, which means employment or service. Ministry wasn't intended just for pastors preaching on Sundays. It was also for those who take care of clients, students, customers, or patients every day.

Each and every job is a ministry because God equips us and calls us to do the job. And by doing so, we are glorifying Him. By being followers of Christ, we are expected to minister and support everyone everywhere—which means not only in your home but also in your workplace, and everywhere else. As Gordon Smith puts it in *Courage and Calling: Embracing Your God-Given Potential,* "We need to thunder from our pulpits and celebrate at every turn in the life of the church that God is calling people into education, the arts, public office, business, engineering, medicine, the service professions—quite literally into every area and sector of human life."[18]

As Peter writes,

> As each has received a gift, use it to serve one another, as good stewards of God's varied grace: whoever speaks, as one who speaks oracles of God; whoever serves, as one who serves by the strength that God supplies—in order that in everything God may be glorified through Jesus Christ. To him belong glory and dominion forever and ever. Amen. (1 Peter 4:10–11)

Peter tells us that we should go into every area and use whatever spiritual gifts we have received. This is not just pastors, but each of us.

Don't Be Lazy

God doesn't want us to be lazy. Work is a gift from God. After creating Adam, the first thing God did was give him a job: "The Lord God took the man and put him in the Garden of Eden to work it and keep it" (Genesis 2:15). God created work. It's part of His plan for us. Work was God's design for us from the very beginning. Even if you don't love your job, you should view it as a gift.

Jesus was a carpenter, and His earthly dad, Joseph, was too. Even God got His hands dirty when he created man out of the dust of the ground. So you could say we are hardwired for work since we are created out of God's image. We should have a desire to create and a desire to work.

My dad was old-school. He worked hard and long every day. He owned a service/gas station and got up at 5:00 every morning to have the station open at 6:00. He did that six days a week. He would be home for dinner, but every night at 9:00 he had to go back to the station to read the pumps and collect the money. I remember him and my mom doing payroll at the dining room table once a week late at night so they would have their employee's paychecks ready for the next morning. My dad did payroll long-hand on paper, deducting taxes and social security. My brothers and brothers-in-law all worked at the station at one point in their lives. It was a family business, and it gave me a model of how to work hard and love what you do.

Paul scolds Christians who aren't working in 2 Thessalonians 3:10–12: "For even when we were with you, we would give you this command: If anyone is not willing to work, let him not eat.

For we hear that some among you walk in idleness, not busy at work, but busybodies. Now such persons we command and encourage in the Lord Jesus Christ to do their work quietly and to earn their own living." He is reprimanding those who refuse to do something to deserve their lot in life.

Believers are not to be lethargic. An active Christian is a reflection of an active God who created the universe and continues to work in our lives. We are to do honorable and hardworking labor in all we do.

Standing Out

How should we stand out as Christians in the workplace? We're supposed to be different in life. Does that mean at our place of employment also? The answer is yes, definitely. If we work in the secular world, it is a great chance to be a public witness for our love of the cross. We can stand out in these three ways.

1. Care about others. This sounds so basic, but in this cutthroat, dog-eat-dog world, being compassionate with others at our jobs will really make us stand out and be lights to others. Ask people about their weekends, remember their family members' names, ask co-workers to lunch. Driven by God's love, we can show love by attending a co-worker's wedding or bringing a meal to someone struggling. Serve those around you. Be generous with your time and advice. Don't be too busy to lend an ear to listen to good, or bad, news.

2. Be composed and unruffled. Showing the peace that passeth all understanding during hectic, frantic deadlines is a true indication of the Holy Spirit within us. How we respond during tricky times is a show of our character. When our identity is as a child of God, everything else falls

into place. How we respond to promotions or bonuses, or lack thereof, shows where we find our true hope.

3. Share your faith. Don't be silent about it. Be genuine. "I had a great weekend. Let me tell you about our pastor's sermon," is a great way to respond when someone asks how your weekend was. Look for opportunities to show God's greatness. We can't keep quiet about His love and compassion in our lives. Share what He's done for you.

Making Ends Meet

Obviously, we have to work to provide for our families. There may be days, weeks, or months that you wonder, *How on earth will I make it through? How will I pay the mortgage, put food on the table, and gas in the car?* I've been there, and it makes a person feel anxious. Most of that apprehension comes from not trusting in the Lord's goodness. But He will provide. God has constantly spread a blanket of provision over me and my children.

I remember one particularly tight month. I had $20 until payday, which was three days away. I went to the mailbox after work and there was a blessing from a friend: a check for $50 "just because," it said on the memo line. God appears when we don't even expect him to.

When reading John 6:5–14, pay attention to Philip.

> Lifting up his eyes, then, and seeing that a large crowd was coming toward him, Jesus said to Philip, "Where are we to buy bread, so that these people may eat?" He said this to test him, for he himself knew what he would do. Philip answered him, "Two hundred denarii worth of bread would not be enough for each of them to get a little." One of his disciples, Andrew, Simon Peter's brother,

> said to him, "There is a boy here who has five
> barley loaves and two fish, but what are they for
> so many?" Jesus said, "Have the people sit down."
> Now there was much grass in the place. So the
> men sat down, about five thousand in number.
> Jesus then took the loaves, and when he had given
> thanks, he distributed them to those who were
> seated. So also the fish, as much as they wanted.
> And when they had eaten their fill, he told his
> disciples, "Gather up the leftover fragments, that
> nothing may be lost." So they gathered them up
> and filled twelve baskets with fragments from the
> five barley loaves left by those who had eaten.
> When the people saw the sign that he had done,
> they said, "This is indeed the Prophet who is to
> come into the world!"

Philip automatically goes logical on Jesus. He says, "Eight months of wages wouldn't be enough to feed all these people!" Sometimes our situation might seem overwhelming. Logically the dollars may not stretch, and we're like Philip gazing out at the mass of people with no plan to feed them. But Jesus *always has a plan*. He will always show His awesome provision in the most remarkable way. By using a boy with five loaves of bread and two fish, Jesus not only made it enough, He created an abundance.

Just like my check in the mail, Jesus will use people you'd never expect to show up—and show up big—in your life. He will take your barley loaves and fish, and create a full meal of provision and abundance for you.

If you need help learning to budget and beat debt, Dave Ramsey is the man. He has a proven plan for financial success and is America's trusted voice on money. He shows you how to build wealth God's way. He has changed people's lives since 1992 on his radio talk show and through his books. Definitely check him out at daveramsey.com.

Is It Time to Make a Switch?

Is your dream job not your dream job anymore? Do you have the Sunday night blues every night of the week? We've all been there. Is it just your heart needs tweaking, or is God pulling you in another direction? Here are some things to do if you find yourself in this position.

1. Start praying for direction. God often does close doors to open other doors. So wake up early and start praying. Put it in your prayer journal.
2. Decide that you are going to excel in your job. After all, God put you there, right? Do everything to focus your mind on accomplishing God's will while doing your job. Having this mindset makes it easier and you may start liking it better.
3. Stay in your Bible, and keep inspiring verses handy to read whenever you can. This will keep you encouraged and make you feel better during your workday.
4. Find something to do in your spare time that you really love doing. Get a new hobby. This will give you something to look forward to.
5. If you can, take a few breaks during work to pray and clear your head.
6. Make changes to your routine by doing the same work but in a different way. Mix it up a little. The things you usually do at the end of the day, do at the beginning.

Even if we don't care for our jobs, God still wants us to carry out excellent, God-glorifying work. We are called to be a reflection of the One we serve as ambassadors of Christ.

Tithing

You may be thinking, *I can barely make ends meet. I certainly don't have anything left over to tithe.* But you have it all wrong. If Christ is first in our lives, we should give to Him first—right at the top of our pay. We're giving in faith. And we're giving because we *want* to, not because we *have* to.

My tithing started out small, $10 a week. Sometimes I didn't know where I would get that $10 from. So I started giving at the top, before I even paid the bills. And the Lord provided each week. The $10 grew from there.

How much you tithe is between you and God. Some people believe in the 10 percent rule. Billy Graham believed this. He said, "We have found in our own home, as have thousands of others, that God's blessing upon the nine-tenths, when we tithe, helps it to go farther than ten-tenths without His blessing."[19]

First Corinthians 16:2 tells us, "On the first day of every week, each one of you should set aside a sum of money in keeping with his income." So from this verse we learn that we should give independently, regularly, systematically, and proportionately.

The important thing to remember is that your tithing is between you and God.

I've always tried to remember that giving is a privilege and not a burden. It should not be out of a sense of duty, but rather out of love for the Lord and a desire to see His kingdom advanced. I don't say to myself, *I have to tithe*, but rather, *I get to tithe.*

Second Corinthians 9:6–7 says, "Remember this. Whoever sows sparingly will also reap sparingly, and whoever sows generously will also reap generously. Each man should give what he has decided in his heart to give, not reluctantly or under compulsion, for God loves a cheerful giver."

If God is our first priority, then we will put Him first. If we are putting ourselves first, then our desires will come first. How awful to have to say to ourselves, *I can't tithe this week because I bought myself that new sweater.* Ugh.

Everything we have belongs to God anyway, He's just letting us use it for a short while. So why not have a great attitude about giving Him back some of what already belongs to Him?

> Bring the full tithe into the storehouse, that there may be food in my house. And thereby put me to the test, says the LORD of hosts, if I will not open the windows of heaven for you and pour down for you a blessing until there is no more need. (Malachi 3:10)

This covenant by God to Israel is both a reminder and an encouragement. It includes promises in response to obedience.

My job was definitely one of the biggest blessings after my divorce. Continuing to see God work all things out in my life was remarkable. I couldn't have imagined what He had in store for me when I prayed the prayer-of-all-prayers.

Having a tea party with my students

8

JOY IN THE FUTURE

AS I SAID in the first chapter, just as God resurrected His son from the grave, He can resurrect your life from the death of divorce. God has a plan, future, and timetable for your life. It will all become apparent in His perfect timing. You simply have to learn how to be patient during these waiting phases.

As I said, I never prayed for specifics from God. I let Him fill in the blanks of my life, and the outcome was amazing. For example, I never prayed for a husband, but after ten years as a single mom, God put the most amazing believer in my life. He was the grandfather of one of my students. Here is what Jim has to say.

> Initially I was attracted to Carol because she showed so much love and compassion to the students in her classroom; in particular, my granddaughter. Of course, I was attracted to her outward beauty, but it was important to me that if

I was to date again, I would date someone that my family would love and would be loved by her. My granddaughter adored her, my daughter adored her, and I felt a sense of peace and godliness in her classroom. She also smiled a lot and was attentive to me when I came into her classroom. All these things seemed to point me to the Christian woman I was praying for God to place in my life.

Jim had been a single dad for five years before we met. He was ready to find someone and had been praying for the Lord to place someone in his life.

Before our date even started, picking Carol up at her home, I felt peaceful in her cozy beach house. She came to the door and invited me in with a big smile. She introduced me to her children. I think my biggest impression of her was when I realized she had made a warm and inviting room for her mom to live with her. This endeared me to her immediately.

On our date, we spent a good amount of time talking about our friends, family, church homes, pastors, and her numerous mission trips. I was totally consumed and I literally phased out those around us. I think we spent three hours just talking…and we had so much in common even though there were a few years between us. For those few hours, I became lost in her, and on my drive home I thought, this just may be the woman God wants in my life.

My kids immediately liked Jim, which is not hard to do because he's kind, funny, and easy to talk to. It was also important that my friends liked him. We had a big dinner where he met most of them.

> I think Ron and Rory were my immediate favorites. First, they were older and I was impressed that Carol had friends that were perhaps close to our parents' ages. I could tell immediately they loved the Lord and loved Carol, and I knew I had to pass their test before this relationship between her and I would progress. And that was okay with me as this is what I would expect from two Christian friends who love and are protective of her. The evening we had dinner at Ron and Rory's with all your friends was especially fun as I got to meet Jack and Hector and their spouses who were not only fun, but were also highly protective of the woman they grew to love and wanted the best for. All of her friends were naturally inquisitive of me as they wanted and prayed for the best for her. Perhaps I'll never quite live up to this but I am having so much fun trying!

Some men might have felt intimidated that I had four children, but not Jim.

> Actually, I was happy to know Carol had children. It was important to me to know that I was seeing a woman who raised children of her own, as I had two children and they meant so much to me. And her ability to make my granddaughters feel so much love because of her experiences raising her own children in a Christian home...another

check of a box on my list of the woman I had been praying for God to place in my life.

My job and mission trips were an important part of my life, and I was glad that Jim embraced them as well.

The first time I met Carol was at her job. I love children and often thought of my second career choice as a teacher. So when I first stepped into her classroom, it reminded me of my childhood education, God-centered with lots of colors, fun centers of activity, and hugs, encouragement, and "I love you"s. I watched the way my granddaughter looked at her, with admiration, attention, and sweet smiles.

Hearing about Carol's mission trips kinda sealed the deal for me. Knowing that she loved the Lord so much to sacrifice her time to travel around the globe to help others and bring the message of our Lord to lost souls was amazing! I love to travel so this was another thing that endeared me to her, and thinking ahead about the possibilities of doing mission trips together? Blessings![20]

At the perfect time, God put the perfect man in my life. All the blessings the Lord had filled my life with—my children, my job, mission trips, church, friends—all came together and were enhanced by the addition of Jim. After dating a year, he proposed, and we got married ten months later. J

I have seen God come through time and time again for me without fail. He will do the same for you. You will have a great, abundant life because of Him. In His perfect timing, all things will work together for good (Romans 8:28).

Wedding Day

CONCLUSION

As I sit at my dining room table writing this, with my husband in the other room, I marvel at God's greatness. We had a birthday celebration at our house a few days ago, and family and friends filled our home. In between talking, eating, and karaoke, I took time to reflect on everything around me. Only my Creator could have orchestrated it. I love how the Author of my life wrote the chapters. To me, it's a bestseller. It's a beautiful story of healing, love, happiness, peace, and great joy.

God wants *you* to tell a different story, starting today. Divorce is not the end, but the beginning. You too will have the abundant life, found only through Him. Because of Him, you will be stronger, wiser, and full of life. You will share your blessings with others while sharing the wisdom that you received. "In him was life, and that life was the light of all mankind" (John 1:4)

Only through Him will you find your purpose, because after all, *He* created your purpose.

> And we pray…that you may live a life worthy of the Lord and may please him in every way, bearing fruit in every good work, and growing in the knowledge of God. (Colossians 1:10 NIV)

After a divorce, we may question our purposes. But Jesus's life, death, and resurrection can right every wrong and can specifically fulfill our hearts' cries. He is a spring of Living Water that will never run dry. He alone satisfies us and unlocks deep transformation. He created us intricately and knows our hearts' longings. He alone can give us rest and great joy. Remember that faith the size of a mustard seed can move the mountains in your life today. God wants to handle everything for you, so use your faith in all you encounter. I encourage you to allow God to move in your life by following His plan after your divorce. By doing so, Joy will get the last word.

ENDNOTES

1   Daniel Henderson, "Biblical Self-Talk," Strategic Renewal, accessed November 15, 2019, https://www.strategicrenewal.com/biblical-self-talk/.

2   Aaron Menicoff, "What Can We Learn About Prayer from the Way Jesus Prayed," Christianity, accessed December 10, 2019, https://www.christianity.com/christian-life/prayer/5-lessons-from-jesus-on-prayer.html

3   Ruth Bell Graham, *Legacy of a Pack Rat* (Nashville, TN: Oliver Nelson, 1989), page 99.

4   Charles Ellicott, "Ellicott's Commentary for English Readers," Study Light, accessed December 19, 2019, https://www.studylight.org/commentaries/eng/ebc/romans-8.html

5   Leah MarieAnne Klett, "Francis Chan Shares His Tip for a Better Prayer Life," Christianity Today, accessed January 3, 2020, https://www.christiantoday.com/article/francis-chan-shares-his-tip-for-a-better-prayer-life/131362.htm

6   Cymbala, J., & Merrill, D. *Fresh Wind, Fresh Fire: What happens when God's spirit invades the heart of his people* (Grand Rapids, MI: Zondervan, 2018), page 27.

7   Alex Miller, "An In-Depth, Helpful Travel Guide for Single Parents," Upgraded Points, accessed January 2020, https://upgradedpoints.com/travel/travel-guide-for-single-parents/

8   Mel Walker, "What is the Meaning of Iron Sharpens Iron In Proverbs 27:17," Christianity, accessed January 2020, https://www.christianity.

com/wiki/bible/what-is-the-meaning-of-iron-sharpens-iron-in-proverbs-27-17.html

9   Charles Stanley, "How to Find a Church Home," In Touch, accessed January 2020, https://www.intouch.org/Read/how-to-find-a-church-home

10   Charles Stanley, "How to Find a Church Home," In Touch, accessed January 2020, https://www.intouch.org/Read/how-to-find-a-church-home

11   Rocket Admin, "3 Things That Happen When You Connect With People at Church," The Rocket Company, accessed January 2020, https://www.therocketcompany.com/3-things-happen-connect-people-church/

12   D. Marion Clark, "Christian Giving," Reformed Perspectives, accessed February 2020, http://reformedperspectives.org/articles/dm_clark/dm_clark.Acts04.32.35.html

13   Aaron Smith, "Why Americans Use Social Media," Pew Research Center, accessed February 2020, https://www.pewinternet.org/2011/11/15/why-americans-use-social-media/

14   Barna Group, "Two-Thirds of Americans Have Multigenerational Friendships," Barna, accessed February 2020, https://www.barna.com/research/multigenerational-friendships/

15   Bob Ditmer, "Tim Keller on Jesus' Death as an Act of Friendship," Church Leaders, accessed April 2021, https://churchleaders.com/smallgroups/smallgroups-videos/282696-tim-keller-jesus-death-act-friendship-gospel-coalition.html

16   Francis and Lisa Chan, *You and Me Forever: Marriage In Light of Eternity* (Vereeniging : Christian Art Publishers, 2015, page 52.

17   Jim Daly, "Before You Say You're Not Qualified," Focus on the Family, accessed February 2021, https://jimdaly.focusonthefamily.com/before-you-say-you-39-re-not-qualified/

18   Julia Powers, "Why Every Job is Ministry," InterVarsity, accessed March 2020, https://intervarsity.org/blog/why-every-job-ministry

19   BGEA Staff, "Does a Christian Have to Tithe?" Billy Graham Evangelistic Association, accessed March 2020, https://billygraham.org/answer/does-a-christian-have-to-tithe/

20   Direct quotations used with permission from Jim Schreiber.